GROW YOUR OWN
BASIL

BY LISA J. AMSTUTZ

PEBBLE
a capstone imprint

Published by Pebble, an imprint of Capstone
1710 Roe Crest Drive, North Mankato, Minnesota 56003
capstonepub.com

Copyright © 2025 by Capstone. All rights reserved. No part of this publication may be reproduced in whole or in part, or stored in a retrieval system, or transmitted in any form or by any means, electronic, mechanical, photocopying, recording, or otherwise, without written permission of the publisher.

Library of Congress Cataloging-in-Publication Data is available on the Library of Congress website.
ISBN: 9780756589486 (hardcover)
ISBN: 9780756589592 (paperback)
ISBN: 9780756589523 (ebook PDF)

Summary: Readers follow clear instructions and photos to grow their own basil plant. An easy recipe for a salad and a simple explanation of how plants grow are included at the end of the book.

Editorial Credits
Editor: Erika L. Shores; Designer: Heidi Thompson; Media Researcher: Jo Miller; Production Specialist: Tori Abraham

Image Credits
Shutterstock: Artem Stepanov, 7 (right), 11 (left), brizmaker, 12 (window), Danita Delimont, 19, Elusive Edamame, 17, Food Impressions, cover (top, soil), 6-7 (bottom), GSDesign, back cover, 1, Hunter Leader, 23 (top right), InFocus.ee, cover (bottom), 16, ioanna_alexa, 15 (basil), Kseniia Perminova, 21, Mallinka1, 23 (top left), Mega Pixel, 9, 11 (right), 12 (pot), Melih Evren, 10, Mostovyi Sergii Igorevich, 13, NatalyaBond, 5, Pixel-Shot, cover (right), robuart, 23 (bottom), Skyliz, 15 (finger), Thammasak Lek, cover (top, trowel), 6 (top), Trong Nguyen, cover (middle), 6 (bottom), Vitaly Korovin, 7 (left)

The publisher and the author shall not be liable for any damages allegedly arising from the information in this book, and they specifically disclaim any liability from the use or application of any of the contents of this book.

Any additional websites and resources referenced in this book are not maintained, authorized, or sponsored by Capstone. All product and company names are trademarks™ or registered® trademarks of their respective holders.

Printed and bound in China. 6097

TABLE OF CONTENTS

Growing Basil 4

What You Need 6

What You Do 8

Take It Further 20

Behind the Science 22

Glossary 24

About the Author 24

Words in **BOLD** are in the glossary.

GROWING BASIL

Basil is an **herb**. It can add flavor to your meals. You can grow your own fresh basil!

It is easy to grow basil indoors. Just follow these six steps!

WHAT YOU NEED

- 6-inch (15-centimeter) plant pot
- potting soil
- **trowel**
- 6 to 10 basil seeds
- spray bottle
- water
- a sunny spot for your plant to grow

WHAT YOU DO

STEP 1

Ready to plant? Start with a clean, dry pot. Scoop up soil with the trowel. Put it into the pot. Leave an inch of space at the top.

STEP 2

Sprinkle the seeds onto the soil. Push them down. Cover them with a thin layer of soil.

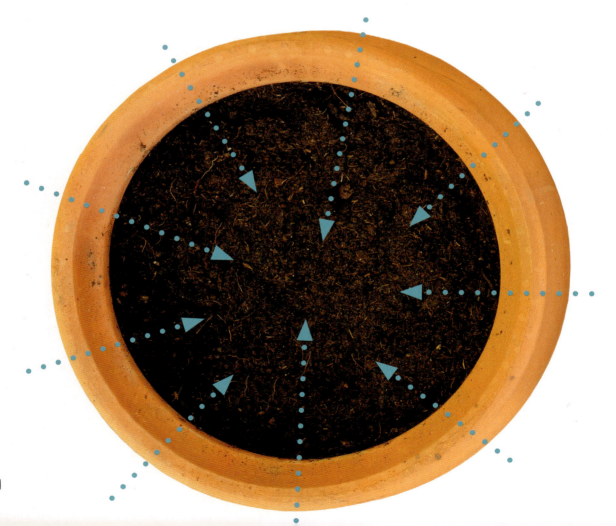

Then fill your spray bottle with water.
Mist the soil well.

STEP 3

Set the pot in a sunny spot. Basil likes a lot of light. It needs six hours per day.

Soon the seeds will **sprout**. They need space to grow. Choose a few to keep in the soil. Pull out the rest.

STEP 4

Check the soil every day. Touch it with your finger. Does it feel dry? If so, mist the soil with water. Keep the soil damp. If the soil dries out, the plants may die.

STEP 5

Basil grows fast. In a few weeks, it will be ready to **harvest**. Cut off some leaves or stems. Not ready to use them? Store cut stems in a jar of water.

STEP 6

Let some leaves grow. Don't pick them all! Pinch off any flower **buds**. Then the plant will keep growing. Basil can grow for a long time.

You can grow basil in a garden too. Plant seeds in spring. Space them 6 to 12 inches (15 to 30 cm) apart.

TAKE IT FURTHER

Now it is time to eat your basil! You can add it to soups or sauces. Put chopped leaves on pizza. Or try making this easy salad:

- 2 to 3 small tomatoes, sliced

- handful of fresh basil leaves

- a few small slices of mozzarella

- drizzle of Italian dressing

- salt and pepper to taste

Mix well and enjoy!

BEHIND THE SCIENCE

Green plants don't need to eat. They make their own food! They need light, water, and air. They need **nutrients** from soil too.

Plants get energy from the sun. They use it to break down water and a gas in the air. This makes a kind of sugar. Plants use this sugar to grow.

GLOSSARY

bud (BUHD)—a small shoot on a plant that grows into a leaf or a flower

harvest (HAR-vist)—to pick a ripe vegetable, fruit, or other crop

herb (URB)—any plant with leaves, seeds, or flowers used for flavoring food, medicine, or perfume

mist (MIST)—to spray lightly

nutrients (NOO-tree-uhnts)—parts of food, like vitamins, that are used for growth

sprout (SPROUT)—to start to grow

trowel (TROU-uhl)—a tool used to scoop up soil

ABOUT THE AUTHOR

Lisa J. Amstutz is the author of more than 150 children's books on topics ranging from applesauce to zebra mussels. An ecologist by training, she enjoys sharing her love of nature with kids. Lisa lives on a small farm with her family.